THE SPANISH THEORY OF EMPIRE
IN THE SIXTEENTH CENTURY

THE SPANISH
THEORY OF EMPIRE
IN THE
SIXTEENTH CENTURY

BY

J. H. PARRY

OCTAGON BOOKS

A DIVISION OF FARRAR, STRAUS AND GIROUX

New York   1974

First published 1940

Reprinted 1974
by permission of Cambridge University Press

OCTAGON BOOKS
A DIVISION OF FARRAR, STRAUS & GIROUX, INC.
19 Union Square West
New York, N. Y. 10003

Library of Congress Cataloging in Publication Data

Parry, John Horace.
    The Spanish theory of empire in the sixteenth century.

    Reprint of the 1940 ed. published by The University Press, Cambridge, Eng.

    1. Imperialism. 2. Spain—Colonies—Administration. 3. Spain—Colonies—America. I. Title.

JV4062.P3 1974   325'.346   74-9626
ISBN 0-374-96275-8

Printed in U.S.A. by
NOBLE OFFSET PRINTERS, INC.
NEW YORK, N.Y. 10003

CONTENTS

Preface	*page* vii
I. The Papal Commission	1
II. The Right of Conquest	12
III. The Case for the Encomienda	27
IV. The Case against the Encomienda	44
V. Theory and Practice in the Colonies	57
VI. Imperialism and Sovereignty	70

PREFACE

This essay was a by-product of a year spent in studying the history of colonial Spanish America, during my tenure of a Charles and Julia Henry Fellowship at Harvard. My thanks are due to Professor C. H. Haring for his constant help and advice during that year; to Professor R. B. Merriman, who first introduced me to Sepúlveda; and to Mr Lewis Hanke, who communicated to me his own enthusiasm for the Spanish writers on the question of empire, and much valuable information about them. I am indebted to Mr Hanke for many of the bibliographical references in this essay, and, more recently, for his kindness in revising and criticising the manuscript before publication.

J. H. P.

I

THE PAPAL COMMISSION

THE Spanish colonial enterprise of the sixteenth century showed all the signs of genuine imperialism—the conviction that the duty of civilised nations is to undertake the political, economic and religious tutelage of more primitive peoples; the eager willingness of government and people to perform this duty and to accept the material rewards involved. The spirit of the Middle Ages had been altogether foreign to imperialism; the nations of Europe were too absorbed in the evolution of their own "personalities" and in the delimitation of their boundaries—their foreign exploits were spontaneous outbursts of youthful energy, producing for the most part only casual and temporary results. The Iberian nations, however, and especially the kingdom of Castile, hardened and aged by centuries of struggle, had achieved long before the rest of Europe centralised government, a stable relation between Church and State, and a developed body of law capable of being imposed wholesale upon a subject people. The government, conscious of its responsibilities, kept a tight hold upon the Indies almost from the first; the *conquistadores*, adventurers, crusaders, quickly gave way to administrators, lawyers and judges, both secular and ecclesiastical. Consequently, at a time when the rest of Europe was fully engaged at home in a triumphant burst of creative effort in science, art and religion, and in the civil wars which attend rapid change and growth, Spaniards occupied themselves in building other Spains across the sea. In the history of the Discovery itself, other nations—the Portuguese and Italians especially—produced great scientists, geographers and navigators; but the greatest conquerors, administrators and lawyers were Spanish.

The deliberate, self-conscious purpose which was so characteristic of the imperialism of the Spaniards and so conspicuously lacking in that of the Portuguese, and later of the British, reflected the immense influence and importance of the Spanish legal profession. Sixteenth-century Spain led the rest of Europe not only in the practice of law and government, but also in the abstract field of jurisprudence. The Spanish jurists, before the middle of the century, evolved a theory of sovereignty distinct equally from the narrow kingship of the Middle Ages and from the unbridled absolutism pictured by Hobbes and his followers. It was, in effect, a theory of a constitutional State, possessed of the right of legislation and unrestricted in its sphere of action, but restricted in its exercise of power by the man-made laws and customs of its subjects. Azpilcueta and Covarrubias, like Bodin later in the century, were no doubt behind their times in describing as constitutional a monarchy which in practice was rapidly becoming more and more absolute. Mariana, later and more observant, noted and lamented the decline of the Cortes; but

THE PAPAL COMMISSION 3

whether or not they noticed the signs of change, a horror of absolutism was common to them all.[1] Throughout the century, books insisting on the legal rights of free peoples, and even in extreme cases advocating tyrannicide,[2] continued to circulate freely, were read without scandal, and exercised a profound influence not only upon thought but upon administration.

In such an atmosphere, the discovery and conquest of a new world naturally gave rise to juridical problems.[3] Perhaps for this reason, as well as through fear of Portuguese competition, the Catholic Monarchs at once demanded Papal sanction for their policy of conquest, and received in answer a series of Bulls confirming not only their sovereignty over discoveries already made—which in Spanish opinion needed no confirmation—but also their right to future discoveries in the same region. The Bulls were not arbitral awards; they were issued by a Spanish Pope who had every reason to be grateful to the Spanish sovereigns. Similar Bulls had previously been granted to the Portuguese; the Bulls of Demarcation of 1493 conferred on the Spaniards rights analogous to those of the Portuguese, and

[1] "...abhorrere prorsus et fugere tenemur absolutae potestatis mentionem...." Didaci Covarrubias a Leyva Toletani, *Variarum ex jure pontificio, regio et caesareo resolutionum*, lib. III, cap. VI.
[2] "...cum principis tyrannide oppressa republica, sublata civibus inter se conveniendi facultate, voluntas non desit delendae tyrannidis...." Mariana, *De rege et regis institutione*, lib. I, cap. VI.
[3] Cf. L. Hanke: *Teorías políticas de Bartolomé de las Casas*. Pub. del Instituto de Investigaciones históricas, LXVII, Buenos Aires, 1935.

limited the area within which the Portuguese rights might be exercised. The revisions and repetitions of the Bulls, to meet Spanish demands, emphasised the importance attached to them by the Spanish monarchs.[1] *Inter Caetera* especially was regarded as the juridical charter of Spanish imperialism, and its chief theoretical defence against intruders from abroad and against interfering humanitarians at home.

Despite Alexander's readiness to meet Isabella's wishes, however, the Bull was not—and could not be —an altogether adequate charter.[2] Of its three most important provisions, the unequivocal grant of "islands and mainlands...towards the West and South...with all their rights, jurisdictions and appurtenances", was held invalid by many Spaniards and by most foreigners. The use of the words "motu proprio" and "plenitudine potestatis" made this part of the Bull inadmissible in France and in England; Henry VII certainly considered himself at liberty to ignore it; Francis I, in a moment of defiance, demanded to be shown the "testament of Adam" which had bequeathed a hemisphere to the Spanish and Portuguese Crowns; while the greatest jurists of the sixteenth century, Vitoria, Suárez, Soto, themselves Spaniards, emphatically denied any papal claim to dispose of the temporal possessions of infidels—the Bull itself excepted lands held by

[1] Cf. H. Vanderlinden, "The Bulls of Demarcation", *Amer. Hist. Rev.* October 1916.

[2] Cf. E. Staedler, "Die *Donatio Alexandrina* und die *Divisio Mundi* von 1493", *Archiv für katholisches Kirchenrecht* (Mainz, 1937), bd. 117, pp. 363–402.

Christians. The supplementary provision, drawing an imaginary line of demarcation between the Spanish and Portuguese spheres of activity, was superseded in 1494 by the Treaty of Tordesillas,[1] which certainly could not be held to bind third parties. There remained only the papal commission to the Spanish Crown to attempt the conversion and education of the natives. No Catholic—and discussion of these matters was long confined to Catholics—ever denied the legality of this commission; but dissension arose at once over the question of what rights, of a temporal nature, might be deduced from it. Did the duty of conversion involve the right of conquest?—the deposition of native rulers, if indeed the Indians had legitimate rulers? the seizure of their lands? the assertion of Spanish sovereignty over their former subjects? And if the Indians should be reduced, by a just conquest, to the position of vassals of the Spanish Crown, what legal and political rights remained to them? Should they be "converted" by force? Might they be enslaved, or robbed of their property? Were they subject to Spanish courts of law, civil and ecclesiastical? Above all, what justification could be found for those all-important institutions, the *encomienda* and the *repartimiento*? The attempt to answer these questions involved a statement on the part of each writer of the nature of papal and imperial authority;

[1] The Portuguese tried unsuccessfully to revive the line of Alexander VI in the 1520's in order to establish their claim to the Moluccas.

of the force of "natural law" and the "law of nations" in determining the grounds for just war; of the efficacy or inefficacy of force in the work of converting the heathen; and of the status, character and capacity of the Indians themselves.

The last was the greatest ground of contention and the greatest source of ignorant speculation. The colonists, faced first with a hostile population, then with a labour problem in a climate unfitted for white labour, naturally emphasised the apparent idleness of peoples accustomed to subsistence farming, and threw in the abusive epithets inseparable from imperialist ambition. Oviedo, the official chronicler of the Indies, declared the natives in general to be "lazy and vicious, melancholic and cowardly...a lying and shiftless people". Many of the Dominican friars, on the other hand, insisting on the purely spiritual nature of the Spanish enterprise, exaggerated both the capacity and the lovable nature of the Indians. Las Casas, the Apostle of the Indians, represented the extreme view in maintaining in his *Apologética Historia* that the Indians fulfilled all the requirements laid down by Aristotle for the Good Life. From such conflicting and interested reports lawyers, theologians and statesmen in Spain endeavoured to generalise upon the character, legal status and rights according to the "Law of Nations", of a collection of peoples ranging from the truculent cannibals of the Lesser Antilles to the cultivated city-dwellers of the Yucatan peninsula.

The Crown, torn between its conscience (elastic

THE PAPAL COMMISSION 7

under Ferdinand) and its rents, eagerly collected opinions and sought by all possible means to justify the American enterprise by legal and philosophical pronouncements. In 1510 the distinguished jurist Palacios Rubios, of the Council of Castile, was ordered to draw up the *Requerimiento*, calling upon the Indians to submit peacefully and to receive the Faith—a solemn legal document which was to be read aloud to the Indians on all occasions before military operations might be undertaken against them. The obligation was taken literally, if not always seriously: as late as 1542 the Viceroy, Antonio de Mendoza, ordered the Requerimiento to be read to the rebellious Caxcanes, encamped in the peñoles of Mixton and Nochistlán. The reading was made in the Spanish language and was entrusted to a friar who, according to the chronicler Tello,[1] was compelled to stand out of range of arrows and slingshots, and presumably, therefore, out of earshot; but the requirements of law and justice were held to have been fulfilled. The seventh clause of the Requerimiento recommended the Indians to devote time and thought to the theological views propounded, before making their reply. Oviedo,[2] referring to a similar but earlier occasion, commented ironically upon this requirement: "I would have preferred to make sure

[1] Tello, *Crónica Miscelánea*, cap. CXXXVII. The Text of the Requerimiento is in the *Colección de documentos inéditos...de América y Oceanía...del Real Archivo de Indias*, Pacheco and Cárdenas ed. (Madrid, 1864–6, referred to as *D.I.I.*), vol. III, p. 369.
[2] Oviedo, *Historia General de las Indias*, lib. XXIX, cap. VII.

THE PAPAL COMMISSION

that they understood what was being said; but for one reason or another, that was impossible... I afterwards asked Doctor Palacios Rubios, the author of the Requerimiento, whether the reading sufficed to clear the consciences of the Spaniards; he replied that it did, if carried out in the correct form."

In the sphere of government, also, high-sounding formal declarations were common, and served to legalise an existing state of affairs. In practice the early colonial decrees confirmed piecemeal the rough systems of administration established by the colonists themselves—systems based, if not on slavery, at least on the *encomienda* and the *repartimiento*. An encomienda[1] was a group of Indian villages "commended" to an individual Spaniard—the *encomendero*—who undertook the obligations of military service, the instruction and protection of his Indians, and the maintenance of clergy in the villages. In return, the encomendero was entitled to support himself and his household by levying tribute from his charges—tribute which in the early days frequently took the form of free forced labour. Villages not assigned to encomenderos—left "en cabeza de Su Magestad"—paid their tribute to the Crown. After the extension of the Spanish power on the mainland, these Crown pueblos were subjected to a distinct form of labour assessment known in New Spain as *tanda* or *repartimiento*[2] and in Peru as *mita*,

[1] Cf. Zavala, S., *La Encomienda Indiana* (Madrid, 1935).
[2] Cf. *Recopilación de Leyes de Indias*, vi, xii, 20, 21, 22, 23, 24, 25, 27, 29, 30, 33; vi, xv, 3, 4, 5, 6.

THE PAPAL COMMISSION

according to which each pueblo supplied a definite number of labourers every week, to be employed at a fixed wage by the Spanish settlers, under the supervision of a local magistrate detailed to perform this duty. Neither encomienda nor repartimiento affected the title by which Indians held their cultivated lands;[1] nor was the enslavement of Indians permitted, except in the case of prisoners of war. In theory the right to provide encomiendas and repartimientos belonged to the royal prerogative, though some at least of the conquistadores granted encomiendas to their followers and sought royal confirmation afterwards.

Some system of forced labour was essential in the early stages, for the profitable use of the land and for the working of the mines. From the point of view of the Crown, the repartimiento was a far more satisfactory institution than the encomienda. The encomenderos, however, quickly became too powerful to be easily dispossessed; while close intercourse with a Spanish overlord was considered necessary for the instruction and conversion of the natives, and for the protection of the missionary friars—who, however, in many cases indignantly repudiated such protection.

The encomienda received its first legal recognition in the instructions sent to Nicolás de Ovando, governor of Española, in 1503.[2] From about 1510,

---

[1] Cf. Zavala, S., *La propiedad territorial en las encomiendas de Indios*, Universidad, vol. IV, no. 20 (Mexico, 1937).

[2] *D.I.I.* vol. XXXI, pp. 209–12.

the Dominican order began its agitation at the Spanish court for the reform of colonial government and especially for the abolition of the encomienda. The Laws of Burgos, however, the first Spanish colonial code, merely reiterated earlier provisions forbidding personal servitude—since personal vassals of the Spanish Crown might not logically belong entirely to other masters—and restricted the amount and the character of the labour to be exacted by the encomenderos.[1] The disappointment of the reform party after their promulgation was indicated by the sudden return to Spain of the Dominican prior in Española, to complain to the King of the inadequacy of the laws from the theoretical and humanitarian points of view. He received little satisfaction. The Crown continued to issue general edicts against the ill-treatment of Indians, and upon the establishment of Royal Audiencias in the New World, those powerful courts were charged with the task of protecting Indian interests against unscrupulous encomenderos; but the encomienda system remained in force, based in law upon the convenient theory that the Indians were mentally childish or incapable, based in practice upon the common interest of the colonists and the royal treasury.

The New Laws of 1542—the only radical and comprehensive attack ever made upon the system, by a conscientious monarch under the influence of humanitarian theorists at court, came near to plung-

[1] Cf. Text of Laws of Burgos, printed in L. B. Simpson, *The Encomienda in New Spain* (Berkeley, 1929).

ing the colonists into civil war, and produced a controversy whose bitterness reflected on a small scale the religious schism raging outside the Spanish borders. The enactment of the New Laws came as a startling revelation to those whose interests lay in the colonies, of the power of theoretical argument to influence colonial legislation. Public attention was directed to the deliberations of theorists. The deliberations themselves, moreover, changed subtly in character; in the earlier days of American settlement the subject of imperialism had been handled to some extent objectively; writers for the most part set themselves the task of justifying the entry of the Spaniards into the New World, and the fact of political dominion there, according to natural law and the Scriptures. Towards the middle of the century the writings became more polemical; they contained similar arguments, but were essentially concerned with the *nature* of Spanish administration in the Indies, with the conflicting "rights" of native and colonist, and directly or indirectly with the encomienda. The apologists of the encomienda were late comers in the field of theory—firmly entrenched though the institution was in the Indies—since most of the early writers on the subject of imperialism were Dominicans, and the Dominican order supplied the strength of the reform agitation.

II

THE RIGHT OF CONQUEST

THE Dominicans in the early sixteenth century were the principal champions throughout Europe both of missionary enterprise and of scholastic thought. At the Spanish court they held a privileged position—at least under Charles V—as the Emperor's emissaries in his intricate negotiations with the Papacy. In the New World they supplied a body of zealous and disciplined teachers; in Spain, determined and fearless writers upon the theory of Empire. Despite differences among themselves, most of them held steadily to the principles of individual liberty and free conversion, and in this they received distinguished support from outside the order also. About the time of the Junta of Burgos two treatises appeared in Spain on the subject of the Indies, one by the canonist Matías de Paz, a Dominican,[1] the other by the civil jurist, Palacios Rubios,[2] both declaring that the Indians were rational beings, and naturally free both before and after conversion, and that their paganism by itself gave no ground for war against them. Both writers proceeded to qualify this de-

[1] Matías de Paz, *De Dominio Regum Hispaniae super Indios*, extracts printed in *Archivum Fratrum Predicatorum*, III (Paris, 1933). Cf. V. B. de Heredia, *Un Precursor del Maestro Vitoria*, Salamanca, Establecimiento Tipográfico de Calatrava, 1929.

[2] Palacios Rubios, *De Insulis Oceanis*, rediscovered in 1870, not yet published.

claration, however, by restating the doctrine, associated with the name of Henricus de Segusia, Cardinal of Ostia, of universal papal dominion in temporal as in spiritual matters, thus basing the rights of the Spanish conquerors upon a papal grant overriding the "natural rights" of the Indians: "The authority of the Supreme Pontiff alone may give to our Catholic and invincible King the right to govern these Indies, with political, but not despotic, rule, and so keep them perpetually under his dominion."[1] The doctrine of papal sovereignty was a commonplace among canonists of the fifteenth and early sixteenth centuries, while the medieval conception of the world as a homogeneous Christendom with an infidel fringe still lingered. It involved the belief that infidels might retain their lands and possessions only by the favour of the Church. If they should refuse to recognise papal authority, the Pope might direct the steps necessary for bringing them into obedience—even to the extent of appointing Christian rulers over them, with the proviso, however, that such appointed rule might be "politicum" only and not "despoticum". Ostiensis had had in mind the infidels of the Near East. His doctrine as applied by Palacios Rubios to the New World became a confused mixture of humanitarianism, papal absolutism, and Spanish imperialism—the discovery of America had demonstrated more powerfully than any theory the error of regarding "the World" and "Christendom" as more or less coter-

[1] Matías de Paz, *De Dominio*.

minous. From the time of the Junta of Burgos onwards, writers on the subject of the Indies began to admit the absurdity of calling upon the Indians to acknowledge the authority of a Pontiff of whom they had never heard. The more radical theorists sought justifications of the Spanish enterprise which might be independent of papal authority; others, more cautious, hedged the papal grant with legal and humanitarian restrictions.

Gregorio López was the most outstanding representative of the cautious "transition" school.[1] He held that the Spanish Crown derived its rights of conquest from the "apostolic concession", but that the nature of such a concession forbade the use of military force except as a final resort. The Indians should not, at first, be attacked or intimidated; missionaries should be sent among them, to preach the Gospel and to convince them that they had nothing to fear from the Spaniards, and fortresses should be built, both to protect the missions and to form centres of peaceful trade and intercourse. López considered that if the Spaniards showed sufficient wisdom and indulgence at this stage, the Indians would probably submit voluntarily to the Pope in matters spiritual, and to the King in matters temporal. If, however, the Indians attacked the missionaries, punitive expeditions might be sent against them, with the sole object of punishing, or preventing, such unprovoked attacks. The Indians

[1] Cf. Román Riaza, *Anuario de la Asociación Francisco de Vitoria*, vol. III, 119.

might not be attacked for refusal to accept the Faith, or for idolatry; human sacrifice, however, constituted a "casus belli", since it involved innocent victims, and the same argument applied to attempts on the part of pagan Indians to persecute Christian converts. Finally, and most important of all, López firmly rejected that part of the Ostiensian doctrine which enjoined war and confiscation of property against those pagans who refused to accept the authority of the Pope.[1]

The compromise evolved by Gregorio López represented fairly accurately the orthodox official view of the Indian enterprise, as illustrated, for instance, in the Ordinances concerning Discoveries of 1573.[2] The special interests of the Spanish colonists on the one hand, and the enthusiastic humanitarianism of some of the missionaries on the other, called for other and less orthodox arguments; but in Spain, López' views were generally accepted. Covarrubias followed him, as did Solórzano in the *Política Indiana*, in attempting to solve the awkward problem of how to uphold Indian interests, while showing a proper respect for the authority of the Papacy and of the Spanish Crown. The close connection between Church and State in Spain made it especially necessary for Spanish theologians to proceed with caution. Significantly, the first writer to attack the problem by suggesting a secular justification for Spanish imperialism was not a Spaniard.

[1] S. Zavala, *Instituciones jurídicas de la Conquista de América*, p. 96 (Madrid, 1935). [2] *D.I.I.* vol. VIII, p. 484.

The international and relatively objective outlook of early sixteenth-century scholarship was well illustrated by the fact that John Major (or Mair), a Scottish Dominican with no personal or practical interest whatever in the Indies, felt impelled to write in support of the Spanish enterprise, and to begin with an emphatic denial of universal papal sovereignty: "...for the supreme Pontificate was first established by Christ; but He granted no temporal monarchy."[1] This statement was supported by examples of the freedom of the kingdoms of France and Spain from outside interference in temporal matters. The Emperor's claim to universal dominion fared no better than the Pope's at Major's hands; the Emperor was one territorial prince among many, not even qualified to act as an arbiter between European rulers, since at the time when Major wrote he was engaged in war with the King of Hungary. There is more than a suspicion of "modern"—perhaps Scottish—pragmatism in this treatise—for instance, in the statement that "There is no senate in which the partition of kingdoms is discussed; when kingdoms are divided, their boundaries are fixed by the sword— I speak of practical affairs, as they really exist".[2] So much for the two swords! Temporal dominion,

---

[1] *Quartum Sententiarum*, dist. 24, quaestio 3: "Non est unum caput in temporalibus, cui reges sunt subiecti omnes...nam primo summus pontificatus est ex institutione Christi: nulla tamen monarchia in temporalibus est ex ejus institutione." Cf. P. Leturia, *Maior y Vitoria ante la Conquista de América, Estudios Eclesiásticos* (Madrid, 1932). Father Leturia prints, as an appendix, the relevant passages from Major's *Sententiae*.

[2] Leturia, *op. cit.* Appendix.

according to Major, was founded not in faith and charity, but in natural law. By that law infidel princes held their office by as good a title as any Christian, a title which neither Pope nor Emperor might dispute, if the infidel's only offence were his infidelity.

A justification for the Christian conquest of the lands of infidels arose at once, however, if the heathen refused to tolerate the peaceful preaching of the Gospel. Major, like Palacios Rubios, was thinking here of the infidel of the later Middle Ages. The Mongols had permitted preaching in their territories; Dominican and Franciscan missions had made converts without interfering with the temporal and heathen lordship of the great Khans. In the fifteenth century the Mongols had given place to the Ottomans, a militant and military Moslem power, with whom no argument was possible except that of the sword. The problem in Major's mind was whether the Indians were, so to speak, Mongols or Ottomans; if, as it appeared, the Indians had behaved as Turks and resisted peaceful missionaries by force of arms, contrary to natural and divine law, then the Spaniards had sufficient justification for deposing the native rulers and seizing power themselves. Of these questions the Pope was judge, by virtue of his "regulating" authority over Christian princes in matters pertaining to the Faith. He might delegate missionary work among obstinately heathen peoples, and might if necessary authorise the seizure of political power and the levying of tribute, to cover the cost of supporting the missionary preachers by armed force. Here, so early in the sixteenth century, was the doctrine of indirect power especially associated with the name of Cardinal Bellarmine, but evolved by the Dominicans long before Bellarmine's time. Juan de Torquemada had suggested it. Major used it as the basis of his theory of conquest, and Vitoria was to elaborate it into a juridical system.

All this was good sixteenth-century thought, and Major was on safe ground. At this point, however, his thought took a curious turn which made him a precursor of Sepúlveda as well as of Vitoria and Bellarmine. Leaving his theological ground, he found a second justification of conquest in the duty of bringing civilisation—in a secular sense—to a barbarous people. Aristotle, naturally, was his authority, quoted with all the affectionate familiarity of the medieval schoolmen, who spoke always as if they held "our philosopher" firmly by the arm. But though the argument was ancient, its imperialist application was modern: "Those people live like animals...it is evident that some men are by nature free, and others servile. In the natural order of things the qualities of some men are such that, in their own interests, it is right and just that they should serve, while others, living freely, exercise their natural authority and command."[1] Major was the first publicist to apply the Aristotelian theory of natural servitude to the natives of the New World or to any entire race. Sepúlveda, a confirmed imperialist,

[1] Leturia, *op. cit.* Appendix.

THE RIGHT OF CONQUEST 19

quotes him as an authority in his "Apologia pro libro de justis belli causis";[1] but Sepúlveda shrank from the full implications of the theory—Major did not. The theologian Major, despite his rejection of Ostiensis, thus arrived at a theory of colonisation and conversion far harsher than that of the lawyer Palacios Rubios—a theory of wholesale servitude.[2]

More humane, more logically complete, and far more pregnant with consequences for the future, were Francisco de Vitoria's *Relectiones de Indis*. Vitoria himself denied having seen any previous treatise upon the question of the Indies.[3] The works of Matías de Paz and Palacios Rubios were never published; but Vitoria was certainly familiar with some parts of Major's *Commentaries*, and in writing of the Indies he followed Major in three fundamental arguments. Both denied to Pope and Emperor any temporal jurisdiction over other princes, whether Christian or infidel.[4]

[1] *Johannis Genesii Sepúlveda Cordubensis opera*, vol. IV, pp. 340–1 (Madrid, 1780).
[2] It is fair to observe that in 1511 when Major wrote, the sedentary civilisations of the Andes, Yucatan, and the Anahuac plateau, were still unknown to Europeans.
[3] "Ego nihil vidi scriptum de hac quaestione", *De Indis*, II, conclusion. The three *Relectiones de Indis* are printed in an English translation, as an appendix to J. B. Scott, *The Spanish Origin of International Law* (Oxford, 1934).
[4] "Ex quo patet error multorum jurisconsultorum, ut Archidiac., Panormit., Sylvest., et multorum aliorum, qui putant quod Papa est dominus orbis proprio dominio temporali, et quod habet auctoritatem et jurisdictionem temporalem in toto orbe supra omnes Principes. Hoc ego non dubito esse manifeste falsum, cum tamen ipsi dicant esse manifeste verum, ego puto esse merum commentum in adulationem et assentationem Pontificum, unde et cordatiores jurisconsulti oppositum tenent," *De Potestate Ecclesiae*, relectio I.

Both recognised the political dominion and proprietary rights of the infidel in his own land. Both accorded to the Pope a "regulating" authority, recognised among Christian peoples, by virtue of which a single prince might be charged, to the exclusion of others, with the task of protecting missions to the heathen, by armed force if necessary. Apart from these conventional similarities, however, the points of view of the two Dominican writers differed profoundly. Major, despite his appeal to fact and reason, wrote as a theologian and a theorist, interested in the Indies in a purely abstract sense as a field for evangelising and civilising enterprise. The Indians, for him, were a branch of the great body of "the Heathen" and might justly be punished for the sins of those other pagans who had defiled the Holy Places—the conquest of the New World was simply another Crusade. Vitoria, on the other hand, was concerned with the moral and legal aspects of an urgent practical problem—a problem of international relations. In the *Relectiones de Indis*, the Indian races were considered as politically organised peoples, subject, with the peoples of the Old World, to the rules of *Jus gentium*. Vitoria was among the earliest of those thinkers who held that "there was a natural law connection between all nations, and that this connection, while it did not issue in any authority exercised by the Whole over its parts, at any rate involved a system of mutual rights and duties. From this point of view international law was conceived as a law binding *inter se* upon States which were still in a state of nature in virtue of their sovereignty, and binding upon them in exactly the same way as the pre-political Law of Nature had been binding upon individuals when they were living in a state of nature."[1] *Jus gentium* was the law "quod naturalis ratio inter omnes gentes constituit".[2] It was not primarily the idolatry, the wickedness, or the barbarity of the Indians, but their transgressions of this newly conceived international law, which in Vitoria's view gave to the Spaniards any right which they might possess to conquer the lands of the New World.

Vitoria's theory of international justice assumed, though without stating, the now familiar doctrine of the equality of States. The principal rights possessed by every nation were those of peaceful commerce and intercourse with every other nation (provided that no harm were done to the natives of the land visited); and the peaceful preaching of the Gospel. The Spaniards originally shared with other nations the right to visit the Indies upon such errands. The Pope, however, "quia potest ordinare temporalia, sicut expedit spiritualibus", had confided the task of evangelising in the New World to the Spaniards alone, partly as the nation best fitted for the task, and partly to avoid strife, since the Spaniards possessed the subsidiary claim of prior discovery. The papal decree was binding upon all Christian princes, though

[1] Barker, trans.: Gierke's *Natural Law and the Theory of Society*, vol. I, p. 85.
[2] Vitoria's adaptation of Justinian's *Institutes*, I, 2, 1: "...quod naturalis ratio inter omnes homines constituit."

not upon the Indians; but the Indians, equally with the Christians, were bound by the wider rules of the Law of Nations to receive the Spaniards peacefully, and to hear the Gospel even if they would not accept it. Refusal to hear, refusal to admit strangers, the murder of traders and missionaries, would give the Spaniards a just ground for war and conquest—just as later, such resistance was held to justify the political encroachments of the East India Company, though English imperialism emphasised the economic rather than the theological side of the argument. Vitoria met the obvious objection, that resistance might be deliberately provoked, with a moral proviso that the traders must behave as Christians and present the Gospel fairly to the natives. The argument that the Indians incurred the penalty of conquest merely by rejecting the Gospel after hearing it preached—even if valid under any circumstances, which Vitoria doubted—broke upon the fact that Christianity had not been fairly presented in America: "I hear of no miracles or signs or religious patterns of life; but rather of many scandals and cruel crimes and acts of impiety."[1]

The Law of Nations in Vitoria's thought, unlike modern International Law, did not require universal acceptance in order to claim universal validity. The nearest approximation on earth to a formulation of Natural Law (from which, originally, *Jus gentium* was derived) was "a consensus of the greater part of the whole world, especially in behalf of the common

[1] *De Indis*, lectio II, § 14.

good of all".[1] The supposed majority of peoples constituted by Christian Europe was considered, therefore, to be the guardian of Natural Law and to have a secondary right and duty (since the Indians were members of the "natural society and fellowship"—"illi omnes sunt proximi") to exercise a paternal and benevolent guardianship over peoples living in ignorance or open defiance of Natural Law. Typical offences against Natural Law—quite distinct from offences against the Law of Nations—were tyranny, human sacrifice, and bestiality; all of which crimes were attributed by the colonists to the Indians. Vitoria, however, never disposed to accept uncritically the tales of the colonists, hesitated to deduce from this argument a definite right of conquest.

The possibility that a majority of Indians might elect to live under Spanish rule; the duty of protecting converts from the dangers of persecution or relapse, and innocent people from tyrannical rulers; the right of assisting a friendly nation in a just war against a neighbour (such as the war of the Tlascalans against the Aztec confederacy, of which Cortés made such adroit use)—all were recognised as possible minor justifications for Spanish intervention in the New World. Finally, Vitoria suggested that if the Indians were totally irrational beings, it would be a charitable action for the Spaniards to assume responsibility for their government. He never accepted definitely the view that the Indians were "amentes",

[1] *De Indis*, lectio III, § 4.

though he admitted that some of them appeared to be nearly so; but even if such a theory could be proved, the resulting authority of the Spanish Crown would be limited. Here, again, the moralist accompanied the jurist and the theologian, with the warning words: "I make the suggestion (of the irrationality of the Indians) only tentatively, and with this condition: that Spanish rule should be exercised in the interests of the Indians and not merely for the profit of the Spaniards."[1]

Vitoria, pleading his ignorance of American affairs, declined to commit himself over the question of which of the possible justifications of conquest had proved valid in the Indies, though he ventured a tentative general opinion: "The prime consideration is that no obstacle be placed in the way of the Gospel...I personally have no doubt that the Spaniards were bound to use force and arms in order to continue their work there, but I fear measures were adopted in excess of what is allowed by human and divine law."[2] Whatever grounds for just war may have existed in the Indies, however, Vitoria would have preferred an empire based on peaceful trade to one formed by conquest; he believed peaceful commerce to be at least as effective as conquest, not only in spreading the Gospel, but in satisfying a legitimate desire for commercial profit and for the increase of the royal revenues: "The Portuguese, to their own great

[1] *De Indis*, lectio III, § 18. Vitoria was more uncompromising than most modern exponents of the idea of trusteeship. Compare Lord Lugard, *The Dual Mandate* (London, 1920).

[2] *De Indis*, lectio III, § 12.

profit, have a big trade with similar people, without reducing them to subjection...a tax might quite fairly be placed on the gold and silver which would be brought away from the Indies...inasmuch as the maritime discovery was made by our sovereign, and it is under his authority that trade is carried on in safety."[1] Under such an arrangement, the scope of just war would be confined to punishing those who forcibly obstructed the traders and the Christian missionaries.

Vitoria wrote the last outstanding treatise on the question of the theoretical grounds for the Spanish conquest, which dealt with the problem judicially and was not an obvious polemic. His sympathies, however, were evidently with the Reform party. It would be difficult to justify the encomienda on his premises, for even if the Indians were proved to be irrational beings, as the apologists of the encomienda asserted, he believed that the duty of assuming a benevolent guardianship belonged to the Crown and not to private individuals. He was always emphatic in his assertions that no title could be found to justify the enslavement of the Indians or the confiscation of their property, except in the case of prisoners taken in the act of unjust war or rebellion—enslavement in this case being regarded by Vitoria, as by most sixteenth-century writers, as a mitigation of the death sentence.[2] The *Relectiones de Indis* contributed to the solution of the urgent practical problem of the treatment of the Indians, as well

[1] *De Indis*, lectio III, § 18.   [2] *De Jure Belli*, § 42, 46.

as debating the more theoretical question of the justice of the conquest. Vitoria admitted, indeed, that this last question was, by his day, almost purely academic; he remarked with an air of resignation that once the Spaniards were installed in the Indies they could not withdraw and leave colonists and converts to perish.[1] Vitoria's great influence and his considered humanity (which constituted the greatest difference between him and Major) could not fail to affect official thought on the Indian question. His belittling of the imperial authority called forth a reprimand from the Emperor and a strong hint to the Dominicans not to discuss such problems in future, in public; but many of the legal principles for which Vitoria, as well as Las Casas, argued so persuasively, came to be embodied in imperial legislation. The New Laws of 1542, and even more the Ordenanzas sobre Descubrimiento of 1573,[2] both extremely liberal and humane colonial codes for their time, illustrate well the influence which humanitarian theory exercised upon the Spanish Crown throughout the sixteenth century.

[1] *De Indis*, lectio III, conclusion.
[2] *D.I.I.* vol. VIII, p. 484. Complete text of Ordenanzas sobre Descubrimiento 1573. The key to the spirit of the code is in clause XX: "Los descubridores por mar o tierra no se empachen en guerra ni conquista en ninguna manera, ni ayudar a unos Indios contra otros, ni se revuelvan en cuestiones ni contiendas con los de la tierra, por ninguna causa ni razón que sea, ni les hagan daño ni mal alguno, ni les tomen contra su voluntad cosa alguna suya, sino fuere por rescate, o dándosele ellos de su voluntad."

III

THE CASE FOR THE ENCOMIENDA

THE arrival of the second Audiencia in New Spain in 1530 marked the beginning of the official movement to clip the wings of the Conquistadores, and to replace their authority by that of royal justices and officials. Juan de Zumárraga, official Protector of the Indians and first Archbishop of Mexico, had already begun his stern campaign against the abuses of the encomienda; the Junta of theologians and jurists convened by order of the Emperor at Barcelona the previous year had condemned the whole system. The Audiencia itself carried secret instructions to begin the work of abolishing personal service and of placing Indian communities under the care of paid overseers—Corregidores. Ramírez de Fuenleal, the aged President, soon became convinced of the hopelessness of attempting drastic reforms at that time; but the ultimate intentions of the Government were plain—inspired partly by the agitation of the missionaries and partly by jealousy of the quasi-feudal power of the encomenderos. The Papacy also seemed to be taking sides in the growing controversy between colonists and missionaries and to be supporting the cause of the orders and their Indian protégés. Paul III gave enthusiastic approval to imperial cédulas forbidding the robbing or enslave ment of the Indians,[1] and in 1537 issued three Bulls concerning their treatment. The first, *Altitudo Divini Consilii*, placed all matters touching the baptism and spiritual guidance of the Indians under the ordinary jurisdiction of the Bishops, thus depriving the Spanish Holy Office of any authority over Indians—a measure of considerable constitutional importance, and of obvious interest to the Indians (though some of the Bishops, such as Diego de Landa in Yucatan, organised a very effective persecution of relapsed idolaters). The second Bull, *Veritas Ipsa*, was a severe condemnation of Indian slavery. The third, the famous *Sublimis Deus*, condemned as heretical (as Las Casas had declared it to be, many years before) the opinion that the Indians were irrational and incapable of receiving the Faith. The Bulls were emphasised by the brief *Pastorale Officium*, which provided the penalties of excommunication for those who persisted in the condemned opinions and practices.[2]

The history of these enactments is obscure; the energetic Paul III undoubtedly wished to recover some of the authority over the Spanish Church, which his predecessors had granted away. His immediate action in 1537, however, seems to have been inspired by the reports of a fiery Dominican missionary, Bernadino de Minaya, who came to Rome seeking papal sanction for the Reform pro-

[1] E.g. that of Aug. 2, 1530: *Documentos Inéditos...de Ultramar* (Madrid, 1886–7, referred to as *D.I.U.*), vol. x, pp. 38–43.

[2] L. Hanke, "Pope Paul III and the American Indians", *Harvard Theological Review*, vol. xxx, no. 2, April 1937.

gramme.¹ Minaya was rewarded with two years' imprisonment at the command of the Emperor, for the fault of despatching Papal Bulls and briefs to the Indies, without first submitting them to the Council of the Indies for approval. In 1538, moreover, Charles V induced the Pope to issue a further brief which revoked "all other briefs or Bulls issued before, in prejudice of the power of the Emperor Charles V as King of Spain, and which might disturb the good government of the Indies".² The revocation meant that Charles saw in the provision of ecclesiastical penalties in the Indies, a threat to his royal patronage—not that he disapproved of the sentiments expressed in the Bulls (*Sublimis Deus* itself, indeed, was not specifically revoked).³ On the contrary, he approved them, and had already issued decrees (1526, 1530, 1531) emphasising the personal freedom of the Indians and prohibiting the sale or grant of Indian lands to Spaniards. The encomienda and the repartimiento presented a much more formidable problem, being deeply rooted throughout the Indies; but this problem, too, was attacked when, in 1542, Cardinal Loaysa, President of the

¹ Memorial of B. de Minaya to Philip II, 1559 (*Archivo de Simancas*, Estado, Legajo 892, f. 197). Printed in Hanke, *op. cit.*

² According to the official Spanish version, in the Archivo General de Indias. *D.I.U.* vol. XVIII, p. 53.

³ Las Casas used the Bull to support his claims on behalf of the Indians, and personally distributed many copies. Cf. Hanke, *op. cit.* p. 94, and references there. As late as 1584, Fray Gaspar de Recarte cited the Bull in his "Tratado del servicio personal y repartimiento de los Indios de Nueva España". Cf. M. Cuevas, ed. *Colección de documentos del siglo XVI para la historia de México*, p. 356 (Mexico, 1920).

Council of the Indies, with the help of Las Casas and other Dominicans, completed the framing of a legislative code which went far beyond the provisions of Paul III's Bulls.

The New Laws formed a comprehensive code—the first complete and adequate code—for the governance of all the provinces of the Indies.[1] Most of the 1542 provisions duly came into force and were duly included in the great "Recopilación de Leyes" of 1681. They were not, in theory, revolutionary; even the three provisions which struck most directly at the colonists—the absolute prohibition of slavery, even in the mines; the prohibition of the employment of Indians as carriers or in personal service; and the abolition of the encomienda—were not new ideas. What was new and alarming was the urgent determination of the Government to have its instructions carried out, for once, and its apparently irrevocable decision that the encomienda was an anomaly in a centralised monarchy. The old formula, "obedézcase pero no se cumpla", was not to be applied, it seemed, to the New Laws.

The time could hardly have been more inopportune for the promulgation of such a code. In Peru, the distribution of encomiendas among the conquerors was barely completed. In New Spain the Viceroy, Antonio de Mendoza, had just suppressed, with considerable difficulty, the Mixton Rebellion which for

[1] J. García-Icazbalceta, *Colección de documentos para la historia de México*, vol. II, p. 204 (Mexico, 1858–66): "Leyes y Ordenanzas nuevamente hechas...."

THE CASE FOR THE ENCOMIENDA   31

two years had threatened the whole structure of Spanish government in Mexico. The newly appointed Viceroy of Peru obeyed his instructions to the letter, and was faced at once with an armed revolt of the colonists, which quickly grew into a civil war. In New Spain, Mendoza, more prudent, persuaded or frightened the royal visitador, charged with enforcing the New Laws, into postponing their promulgation until further counsel could be taken. Meanwhile protests poured into Spain from colonists who saw themselves deprived of Indian labour and reduced to penury, and from officials and churchmen who feared that the complete liberation of the Indians would encourage further rebellion.[1] These men found, at last, a distinguished theoretical defender, in Juan Ginés de Sepúlveda, who in 1542 wrote his *Democrates Alter*,[2] a full and unequivocal statement of the political theory of sixteenth-century imperialism.

Sepúlveda was running his head into a Dominican wasps' nest. The Dominicans had striven for years to secure the New Laws, and were still smarting under the rebuke of 1539. Cano, and of course Las Casas, wrote violent refutations. Fernándo Váldez, the Chief Inquisitor, on the other hand, held that the book should be broadcast throughout Spain. Per-

[1] E.g. letter to the Emperor from P. Pedro Gómez Maraver, 1544, *D.I.I.* vol. viii, p. 199.
[2] "Democrates Alter, sive de Justis Belli Causis apud Indos", in *Joannis Genesii Sepúlveda Cordubensis Opera* (Madrid, 1780). Printed with Spanish Translation by M. Menéndez y Pelayo in *Boletín de la Real Academia de la Historia*, vol. xxi (Madrid, 1892).

32 THE CASE FOR THE ENCOMIENDA

mission to publish was withheld, and discussion of the question ran on until 1550, when it was submitted, by order of the Emperor, to formal debate in the second Junta of Valladolid, in which Sepúlveda and Las Casas argued face to face. The academic junta was a familiar device for settling points of theological difference; but these men were disputing something more immediate than a point of doctrine or theory.[1] They used the words of Natural Law and the Scriptures, but unlike Vitoria and his predecessors, they twisted them, in each case, to support a practical programme. The opening sentences of the chairman, Domingo de Soto, reflected the same spirit, in pointing out their duties to the members of the learned assembly: "The purpose for which Your Lordships are gathered here...is, in general, to discuss and determine what form of government, and what laws, may best ensure the preaching and the spreading of our Holy Catholic Faith in the New World;...and to decide what organisation is needed to keep the peoples of the New World in obedience to the Emperor's majesty, without damage to his royal conscience, and in conformity with the Bull of Alexander."[2] Passionate pleading was to be expected from Las Casas, who had been fighting in the

[1] Las Casas at times was almost indifferent to points of doctrine; he wished, for instance, to publish the *De Insulis Oceanis* of Palacios Rubios, for the sake of its humanitarian sentiments, despite its support of the Ostiensian doctrine, which Las Casas believed to be heretical.

[2] Olivart, ed., *Aquí se contiene una...disputa...entre...Las Casas...y Ginés de Sepúlveda...* with life of Las Casas (Madrid, 1908).

THE CASE FOR THE ENCOMIENDA

same cause since 1515; but Sepúlveda too, great humanist, master of scholastic method, the friend of Erasmus, despite his judicial air, his perfect style and restrained bearing,[1] became passionate over the rights of the colonists, and passionate in defence of his own proud concept of the mission of a civilised aristocracy.

The foundation of Sepúlveda's thought on the Indian question was his highly original view of natural law—a view coloured by Renaissance humanism, which led him further away from theological ground than any other Spanish thinker of his time. The Ciceronian definition, which "Democrates" quotes, was orthodox enough—"est igitur lex naturae, quam non opinio, sed innata vis inservit". But this "innata vis" could manifest itself in two different ways. In the physical sense, "jus naturale est, quod natura omnia animalia docuit"—for example, such precepts as the duty of reproduction, or of repelling force by force. On the other hand, "innata vis" had a rational implication, as in the definition of Saint Thomas: "Lex naturalis est participatio legis aeternae in creatura rationis compote." This was the law, according to Sepúlveda, which impelled men to respect their parents, to seek good and avoid evil, to keep pledges and to believe the teachings of true religion. If man was by nature

[1] In writing to Cano, for instance, upon the question of slavery, after *Democrates Alter* had been brutally criticised by Cano, "Sed haec viderint doctiores; ego nihil statuo pro certo et definito": cf. A. F. G. Bell, *Juan Ginés de Sepúlveda*, in Hispanic Notes and Monographs (Oxford, 1925).

rational, then the second form of law was as "natural" as the first; but in practice the two forms might conflict. A contradiction appeared in Sepúlveda's thought, therefore, which became more difficult to resolve as he narrowed the circle of what he called "rational" mankind. The contradiction had troubled most medieval thinkers, and had been smoothed over in one way or another by them; but logically, Sepúlveda's thesis required the complete identity of the two laws. Actually, the rational aspect of natural law was always uppermost in his mind.

Natural law as reason was identified in Sepúlveda's thought with *Jus gentium*, the body of rules supposedly common to all organised peoples.[1] Sepúlveda, unlike Vitoria, admitted no secondary law of nations, no rudimentary international law prescribing the natural and proper relations between different peoples. The law of nations, or natural law (he used the two terms almost indifferently), was for him the product of human reason; reason impelled men to obey the Decalogue, the foundation of all law; reason enabled them to evolve, or in the medieval sense to "apperceive", whatever subsidiary laws might be right and necessary, and to formulate a common opinion on all matters of universal importance. In writing of just war, for instance, he remarked that the conquests of the Greeks and Romans were undertaken "...cum magna hominum appro-

[1] Cf. M. García-Pelayo, *Juan Ginés de Sepúlveda y los problemas jurídicos* (Tierra Firme, vol. II, no. 2, Madrid, 1936) and references there.

batione, quorum consensus naturae lex esse putatur".[1]

Sepúlveda did not rely, however, upon the reason of all men, or even upon that of the "greater part", as did Vitoria. His law of nations was to be found only among the "gentes humanitiores"—not among those on the margin of civilisation;[2] and even among civilised peoples, the duty of declaring what was or was not natural law, was confined to the wisest and most prudent men of the higher races. The whole theory was a plea for natural aristocracy—the government of the lower races by the higher, of the lower elements by the higher in each race. Sepúlveda even denied that a people might strictly be considered to have legitimate rulers—in modern terms, to be a state—unless it were governed according to the opinions of its best citizens; though for purposes of maintaining the peace, natural law enjoined obedience even to bad rulers, and rebellion could have no legal justification against a prince whose title was legitimate according to the particular laws and customs of his people.[3]

The corollary of natural aristocracy was natural servitude[4]—since the more perfect should hold sway over the less; the Aristotelian theory, inter-

[1] *Dem. Alt.* p. 286 (Boletín de la Academía).
[2] "...ut humanitatem prorsus exuisse videantur". *De Ritu*, II, 5.
[3] *Diálogo llamado Democrates*, cap. 21.
[4] *Dem. Alt.* p. 293: "Eadem ratione (lege naturae) mares in feminas, viri in pueros, ut pater in filios, potiores, scilicet, ac perfectiores, in deteriores et imperfectos imperium tenent."

preted in the same way by Sepúlveda as by Major, received full weight in *Democrates Alter*, and was made to constitute a general mandate for civilised nations to subdue by force of arms, if no other means were possible, those peoples "...who require, by their own nature and in their own interests, to be placed under the authority of civilised and virtuous princes or nations; so that they may learn from the might, wisdom and law of their conquerors, to practise better morals, worthier customs, and a more civilised way of life".[1] Sepúlveda was too restrained a polemist to level at the Indians such a battery of abusive epithets as Oviedo, for instance, had used; but he did assert that the Indians lived in defiance of natural law, and pointed to their very inability to resist the Spanish invasion, as yet further proof of their inferior state[2] and their need of strong and wise government, for their own good (a surprising lapse, for the sixteenth century, into "Machtpolitik").

From these premisses Sepúlveda might have drawn conclusions embodying a purely secular title for Spanish rule in the New World. This he had no intention of doing; the spreading of the Faith appeared as a solemn duty to him as to all his contemporaries—at least in Spain—and though his theological arguments were logically unnecessary in the general development of his thought, they presented no contradictions. "Compelle eos intrare" was the text underlying the missionary theories of Sepúlveda. Forcible baptism he considered unjust and useless;

[1] *Dem. Alt.* p. 356.   [2] *Ibid.* p. 357.

THE CASE FOR THE ENCOMIENDA 37

nor did paganism, by itself, provide a cause for just war; but effective conversion of large bodies of natives was impossible, except after long contact with Christians. The Indians would not accept Christianity immediately, upon the mere word of strangers, nor change their way of life in a few days.[1] In order that they might learn from the missionaries, and prepare themselves for entry into the Church, it was necessary to place them under civilised government and tutelage, with or without their consent. Something of Saint Augustine's doctrine of the relation between Civitas Dei and Civitas Terrena entered into Sepúlveda's thought—the Scriptures needed the protection of the secular sword—the fate of missionaries, in Sepúlveda's own day, in Florida and on the Pearl Coast, provided a tragic example. Civilisation and Christianity went hand in hand; conquest was a religious duty, an act of charity towards ignorant and unfortunate neighbours. The humility of the apostle, however, was missing in Sepúlveda's words. Conversion, he maintained, could not make an Indian the equal of a Spaniard, or entitle him to political independence.[2]

In dealing with the Papacy and the validity of the Bull *Inter Caetera*, Sepúlveda implied, though without stating, the Ostiensian doctrine: "It was laid down by the decree of the Supreme Pontiff that the Spaniards should exercise lawful authority over these

[1] *Dem. Alt.* pp. 360–1.
[2] *Ibid.* p. 362. A modern analogy of this view may be found in the native policy of the Dutch reformed church in S. Africa.

barbarians."[1] Sepúlveda therefore ranked himself with Gregorio López, and differed in this respect from Vitoria and Soto. He maintained, however, that the papal grant referred principally to spiritual affairs, and that although Alexander VI acted within his rights in making a temporal grant, that grant only confirmed to the Spaniards what was probably theirs already, by natural law.[2] Unlike Matías de Paz, therefore, Sepúlveda regarded the papal grant as one title among many, and not as the sole legal basis of Spanish imperialism.

Natural law, which in Sepúlveda's thought coincided on the one hand with divine law as expressed in the Decalogue, and on the other with the law of nations, gave to the Spaniards a well-defined chain of rights of conquest and colonisation in the New World. The principal rights entitling a nation to wage just war were four: the natural right of repelling force by force; the recovery of possessions which had been unjustly taken; the necessity of punishing criminals who had not been punished by their own rulers— since all men were neighbours, and mutually responsible one for another; and the duty of subduing barbarous peoples by force if they refused to submit voluntarily to the government of a superior race.

This last right depended in its turn upon four causes: the naturally servile nature of barbarians, and their consequent need of a civilised master; their

[1] *Dem. Alt.* p. 346. Cf. also *De Rebus Hispanorum Gestis ad Novum Orbem Mexicumque*, Bk. 1, 12 (*Opera*, IV, 2).
[2] *Dem. Alt.* p. 346.

THE CASE FOR THE ENCOMIENDA 39

habitual crimes against natural law; the plight of the subjects of barbarian rulers, who were the victims of oppression, unjust war, slavery, and human sacrifice; and the duty of making possible the peaceful preaching of the Gospel.

All Christian and civilised nations enjoyed these rights and owed these duties. The special rights and duties of Spain in the New World arose from three causes: the natural superiority of the Spaniards over the other European nations;[1] the right of the first discoverer to occupy land (such as the Indies) which had no legitimate ruler; and the decree of the Pope, at once a spiritual commission to convert the heathen, and a temporal grant of legally unoccupied territory.

Almost all the arguments ever cited in favour of imperialism were used by Sepúlveda. Even the purely pragmatic argument of economic development found a place in his work—the Spaniards had introduced beasts of burden into the Indies, had developed the mines, and taught the Indians profitable methods of agriculture. In general, however, economic arguments were despised,[2] as was natural for a theorist in sixteenth-century Spain, and legal and theological ones preferred. Only one important argument was lacking—that of the sovereign right of every State to strategical safety and an adequate

[1] "Has igitur gentes tam incultas...dubitabimus ab optimo, pio, justissimoque Rege...et ab humanissima et omni virtutum genere praestante natione, jure optimo fuisse in ditionem redactas?" *Dem. Alt.* p. 315.

[2] "...Spes est fore, ut brevi pristina et innata parsimonia in patriam consuetudinem revocetur", *Dem. Alt.* p. 306.

supply of raw materials—the appeal to "honour and vital interests".[1] Such an argument, however, is proper to an age in which competitive imperialism and competitive militarism have developed to the full and demand a far greater proportion of a nation's will and strength than they did in the sixteenth century. Sepúlveda made little mention of the glory or the material gains of conquest, and condemned severely those of the conquistadores who were inspired "auri inexplebili cupiditate".

The logic of Sepúlveda's arguments was undeniable—their principal defect was that they tended to prove too much. Many of his contemporaries and most historians since his time regarded him as an apologist for naked slavery. To Las Casas, for instance, he was "acérrimo e injusto adversario de los Indios sin porqué y sin razón voluntaria".[2] Certainly he wrote in ignorance of colonial conditions, and used purely theoretical arguments to support a system which lent itself in practice to appalling abuses. Certainly, also, he admitted the justice of enslaving prisoners taken in rebellion or in the act of unjust war—a right of the conqueror generally admitted at that time. He added to this admission, however, the warning that enslavement was no longer

[1] As presented, for instance, to the League of Nations Commission by the Italian Delegation. Cf. D. H. Miller, *The Framing of the Covenant* (New York, 1928).

[2] Natural servitude, though a useful theory to the colonists, was repugnant, not only to Las Casas, but to most of the Spanish jurists and theologians. The great Suárez disposed of it curtly: "Hactenus tamen, ut existimo, tam barbarae gentes inventae non sunt," *De Fide*, Disp. XVIII, Sect. IV, § 5.

THE CASE FOR THE ENCOMIENDA 41

a reputable practice among Christian peoples, and that many Indians must have resisted in good faith, thinking that they themselves had just cause for war. Many, also, submitted freely to the Spanish invaders. The enslavement of these people was certainly unjust and probably impious.[1] Sepúlveda protested bitterly, in the Apologia, and in private letters, against those who accused him of brutality in this matter.[2] His ideal of colonial government was "to divide the Indians of the cities and the fields among honourable, just and prudent Spaniards, especially among those who helped to bring the Indians under Spanish rule, so that these may train their Indians in virtuous and humane customs, and teach them the Christian religion; which may not be preached by force of arms, but by precept and example. In return for this, the Spaniards may employ the labour of the Indians in performing those tasks necessary for civilised life."[3] As the Indians grew better acquainted with Christianity and European habits, they were to receive greater freedom—"liberius erunt liberaliusque tractandi ministri".

[1] "...in servitutem redigere et bonis spoliare injustum est, ne dicam impium et nefarium. Quos tamen stipendarios et vectigales habere licet pro ipsorum videlicet natura et conditione," *Dem. Alt.* p. 358.

[2] "...Ego igitur, ne te mea sententia, de qua quaerendum est, lateat, hos barbaros non possessionibus et facultatibus spoliandos esse dico, nec in servitutem redigendos, sed Christianorum imperio subjiciendos." *Apologia pro libro de justis belli causis*, § 2, *Opera*, vol. IV, p. 330. "Ut mancipia vero nulli unquam tractari debent, nisi si qui scelere et perfidia, et in bella gerendo crudelitate et pertinacia, dignos sese praebuerint ea poena et calamitate," *Dem. Alt.* p. 364.

[3] *Dem. Alt.* p. 364.

Sepúlveda, then, was not an advocate of unconditional slavery, but of a "mixed and tempered paternal authority". He supported the encomienda, and the rights of those Conquistadores who proved worthy encomenderos. Unlike Vitoria and Las Casas, unlike the Regent Jiménez who had ordered the "social experiments" to be carried out in the early island colonies, Sepúlveda rejected the possibility that the Indians might in time become capable of self-government in a European sense. He could be quoted, therefore, in support of the perpetual encomienda, which was the next claim of the colonists, after the encomienda for one life, and for two, had received legal recognition.

Sepúlveda's work was recognised and appreciated by many of the colonists (the Town Council of Mexico City regarded him as the chief supporter of colonial interests in Spain) and by many observers in Spain. This appreciation did not arise entirely from self-interest.

For those who—even to-day—believe the reports of men like Antonio de Mendoza, the first Viceroy, rather than such catalogues of horrors as Las Casas' *Brevísima Relación*, Sepúlveda's writings must represent a sane and prudent form of imperialism. Given the fact of conquest, and the fact that historical events are irreversible, the encomienda, with adequate supervision, was probably the most serviceable constitutional form under which Indian and Spaniard might live in peace during the first half-century of the colonial period. It left the Indian communities more or less intact;[1] while for the average colonist it represented a form of authority based on proprietary rights, with their attendant duties and limitations, familiar to men coming from Spain, where traces of feudal tenure still lingered. Precisely for that reason, however, it was unpopular in official circles, and among the civilian lawyers. Sepúlveda lost his case before the Junta of Valladolid,[2] and his chances of future preferment, not only because his theory was thought inhumane, but also because it interposed a powerful aristocracy with vested economic rights, between the Indians on the one hand, and the Crown (and the Crown's "alter ego", the Church), on the other. The encomienda, at least in so far as it represented a form of private authority over the Indians, was inevitably repugnant both to a centralised monarchy and to autocratic missionary orders.

[1] Repeated legislation laid down that the authority of the native caciques, so long as it was not oppressive, should be respected: e.g. Instructions to the President of the Audiencia of Los Charcas, Aug. 16, 1563. *Correspondencia de la Audiencia de Charcas*, ed. R. Levillier, p. 574 (Buenos Aires, 1916).

[2] That is, failed to obtain permission to publish his book.

IV

THE CASE AGAINST THE ENCOMIENDA

THE Spanish monarchs did not succeed in abolishing the encomienda in the sixteenth century. The institution had become too deeply rooted, and the remedy came too late, as Las Casas himself admitted.[1] In 1545 the Proctors of the colonists of New Spain obtained from the Emperor the revocation of Article XXX of the New Laws; the old law by which an encomienda might be held for two lives came into force once more.[2] The encomienda legally re-established by the Cédula of Malines was very different, however, from the institution set up by the Conquistadores; from a quasi-feudal authority, it had changed into a form of pension, held, not of right, but by royal favour, and under stringent conditions— stringent, at least, on paper. No legal authority remained to the encomenderos, who were forbidden to reside in their Indian villages, but commanded to live in the same province in order to fulfil their military obligations. Tribute, and not labour, was

[1] "...el remedio se intentó tardamente, y a este se debió que la Encomienda creciera y echara tantas y tan arraigadas raíces... en tanto grado, que ya el Rey con todo su poder, no ha podido en algunos tiempos extirparla." *Apologética Historia*, cit. Zavala, *La Encomienda Indiana*, Madrid, 1935.

[2] Cédula of Malines, 20 October 1545. Puga: *Cedulario*, vol. I, pp. 472–5. *Recopilación de Leyes*, VI, viii, 4.

THE CASE AGAINST THE ENCOMIENDA 45

the essence of the new encomienda, in New Spain at least; villages held in encomienda paid to their encomenderos the tributes which, in other circumstances, they would have paid to the Crown, tributes assessed and as far as possible enforced by the travelling justices of the Audiencias.[1] The task of drawing the Indians into a Europeanised economic scheme was entrusted to a revised repartimiento system, under which the Indians of every village at stated times were to offer themselves for hire, for fixed wages and for fixed periods of work "without force or vexation, except that which may be necessary to make them work".[2] The system left loopholes for abuses. Many encomenderos, no doubt, extorted illegal labour from their Indians; but, in so far as legislation constitutes a guide, the general attitude of the Spanish government towards the Indians made very considerable advances in the direction of humanity in the years immediately preceding and immediately following the Junta of Valladolid. These advances were due in large measure to the agitations of the Dominican order, and especially to those of Bartolomé de las Casas.

The Dominicans had reached Española during the blackest period of Spanish rule in the New World—

[1] Cf. General Provision to the Audiencias 1551. *D.I.I.* vol. XVIII, p. 476: "Porque no es razón, pués vinieron a nuestra obediencia, que sean de peor condición que los otros nuestros súbditos de nuestros reinos; y todas las tasaciones que contra esta nr̄a declaración estuvieren hechas, las enmendad y tornad a hacer de nuevo." Labour was not to be included in the new assessment for New Spain.

[2] *Recopilación*, VI, xii, 1.

the period of the exploitation, and eventual extermination, of the Island Indians under Ferdinand, while the first Franciscan missionaries stood idly by.[1] It was during this period that Las Casas came to the Indies, was refused absolution as an encomendero, and suffered the spiritual upheaval which made him the leader of the Reform movement, the most powerful and most vociferous of all humanitarian agitators. The impression of the average colonist which Las Casas formed in 1515 remained with him throughout his turbulent life.

Las Casas had powerful friends, and his vehemence and persistence caught the ear of the authorities—especially of the regent Jiménez. Most of the early experiments in colonial reform were made at his petition. It was Las Casas who proposed the Jeronymite mission of 1516—an experiment in theocracy; Las Casas who led the unlucky expedition to Cumaná, which was to establish a colony of Spanish working peasants, not of overseers of native labour; Las Casas who, in an ill moment, suggested the replacement of Indian slaves by imported negroes (a suggestion which he afterwards bitterly repented). Las Casas, too, led the triumphant mission in Guatemala which converted the dreaded Land of War into "La Vera Paz"; and Las Casas, as Bishop, celebrated his induction by excommunicating all the encomenderos of Chiapas, in conformity with the Papal briefs, so earning the lasting hatred of Spanish colonists

[1] The position was reversed later, in New Spain, but not at the Spanish Court.

THE CASE AGAINST THE ENCOMIENDA 47

throughout the New World. His was not the life of a theorist. Many of his writings were either bitter denunciations of the colonists—such as the *Brevísima Relación*, which was gleefully translated into English as *Casas' Horrid Massacres* and used as anti-Spanish propaganda under the Commonwealth—or appeals to humanitarian sentiment, a form of writing foreign to the scholastic temper of the sixteenth century. The debate with Sepúlveda and the struggle to defend the New Laws first compelled Las Casas to rationalise and order his opinions. His most positive views of imperialism are in the pamphlets published in Seville in 1552 and 1553[1], and in the assertions and refutations made before the Junta of Valladolid.[2] Las Casas was sufficiently well equipped in learning and in scholastic training to confront the redoubtable Sepúlveda in debate, and though he lacked both the academic polish of his adversary and the judicial detachment of Vitoria, his first-hand knowledge of the Indies more than outweighed these disadvantages. His writings, as might be expected, contain only

[1] Listed in Hanke, *Teorías políticas de Bartolomé de Las Casas*, Publicaciones del Instituto de Investigaciones históricas, vol. LXVII, Buenos Aires, 1935:

1. Brevísima Relación.
2. Aquí se contiene.
3. Avisos y Reglas.
4. Trienta Proposiciones.
5. Este es un Tratado.
6. Entre los Remedios.
7. Tratado Comprobatorio.
8. Principia.

Texts in *Colección de Tratados de B. de Las Casas*, 1552–1553. Photographic reproduction of this very rare collection in *Biblioteca argentina de libros raros americanos*, vol. III, Publicaciones del Instituto de Investigaciones históricas (Buenos Aires, 1924).

[2] *Aquí se contiene una disputa...entre...Las Casas...y Ginés de Sepúlveda...*, with life of Las Casas, ed. Olivart (Madrid, 1908).

48 THE CASE AGAINST THE ENCOMIENDA

scattered references to problems of pure political thought, and those references sometimes inconsistent one with another; but the theory of colonisation and empire in support of which the references were made is clear and definite. Las Casas allowed the colonist no privilege but that of hard work, and no special reward but that of spiritual achievement.

The key to the whole of Las Casas' thought was his insistence upon liberty. He laid down[1] as the essentials of civilised existence that men should live in politically organised communities and should be entirely free; this was his first deduction from Saint Thomas' definition of natural law, which he accepted, as Sepúlveda did. Men required absolute liberty in order that their reason, which naturally inclined them to live in peace together, to seek good and to avoid evil, might be unrestricted. If the free exercise of reason were a right according to natural law, it belonged as well to infidels as to Christians, and not even the Vicar of Christ, in his zeal for the extension of the Faith, might lawfully invade such a right. Las Casas insisted more strongly than any other writer of his century on free and willing conversion; to use any form of coercion in missionary activity was worthy only of Mahomet. He consistently denounced the Ostiensian doctrine as heretical, and maintained that the Pope in ordinary circumstances held no juridical authority whatever over infidels, to punish their sins or to depose their princes: "For what have I to do to judge them also that are without? Do ye

[1] In *Entre los Remedios*.

not judge them that are within? But them that are without, God judgeth."[1]

Las Casas, like Major and Vitoria, admitted the indirect temporal power of the Papacy over Christian princes in matters relating to the spiritual welfare of Christendom. The Pope might lay upon a prince the charge of defending Christians against infidels such as the Turks, who openly attacked the Faith; and in the case of peoples who had never heard the preaching of the Gospel, he might delegate the duty of conversion to whom he chose. To this extent Las Casas attributed the rights of the Spaniards in the Indies to papal commission, and commended the decision of Alexander VI, with a patriotic description of the virtues of the Catholic monarchs which would have satisfied Sepúlveda himself.[2] He distinguished most carefully, however, between the militant heathen of the Old World and the ignorant Indians of the New; only as a last resort, in the case of determined opposition to the preaching of the Faith, would the papal grant involve any title to temporal lordship, or any right to replace the Indians' natural Princes.

Up to this point the theory of Las Casas was almost identical with that of Gregorio López; but for him, as for Sepúlveda, the justification of the Spanish conquest was only a theoretical preface to a practical discussion. He accepted, perforce, the fact of con-

[1] I Corinthians v, 12, quoted in "Aquí se contiene", v.
[2] "La grandeza de la dignidad que es ser reyes de Castilla y León; la gran perfección de las personas reales, que eran y son y deben ser Cristianísimas zelosísimas de la ampliación de la fe...," etc. Tratado Comprobatorio.

quest, however justified. His real concern was not with international questions, but with the nature of the lordship which the Castilian monarchs actually exercised in the New World. Unlike Sepúlveda, he recognised only the rights of the monarchs, as subjects of the papal grant; the colonists he regarded as possessing no rights except as agents of the Crown. His programme of colonial government involved, therefore, not a theory of natural superiority, but a theory of kingship—an older, and in some ways more primitive theory than that commonly held by the contemporary writers of the Spanish juridical school; for while Azpilcueta, Covarrubias and Molina attributed kingship to some form of secular election, Las Casas clung tenaciously to the medieval idea of divine ordination.

The conventional medieval theory of kingship had assumed an authority autocratic but not despotic—an authority bounded by strict limits, but within those limits supreme. The law of God, the rights of subjects according to their station, the laws and customs of the realm, were held alike to be above the power of the king, whose duty it was to protect and enforce them; but in his own sphere of activity, the administration of justice and the protection of rights, the king had no peer. The kingly rank was ordained by God for the sake of justice and was never the property of the man who held it—"non honos sed onus"—but an office, with high and difficult duties. So long as he performed those duties faithfully, and confined himself to them, every legitimate king was entitled to the

THE CASE AGAINST THE ENCOMIENDA

implicit obedience of all his subjects; if he seriously neglected or overstepped them, he became, *ipso facto*, a tyrant. The exact nature of the limits of royal authority, the action which might be taken against a tyrant—if indeed any action were lawful—by the Church, the people, the magistrates, or the tenants-in-chief, were problems which received widely differing answers from different theorists; but in general those writers, who (before the growth of the idea of sovereignty) held the highest view of kingship, were also the most severe in their condemnation of tyranny. The more solemn the trust, the heavier the penalty for abusing it—that was the view of John of Salisbury, the first serious Western theorist to deal with the topic of tyranny and kingship; it was also the view, four centuries later, of Las Casas. He could declare enthusiastically, in the *Erudita Explicatio*,[1] that the king was the health and life of the citizens, just as the soul was the health and life of the body, and as the soul ruled the body and directed the movements of all its members, so the king ruled his kingdom by the exercise of right reason and counsel. Nevertheless, the power which the King held, in Las Casas' view, was not his own, but came from God, was defined by the law, and was to be exercised only in the interest of the common welfare. The subjects of a

[1] Las Casas: *Erudita et elegans explicatio questionis utrum Reges vel Principes jure aliquo vel titulo, et salva conscientia, Cives ac Subditos u Regia Corona alienare et alterius Domini particularis ditioni subjicere possint.* Published posthumously at Frankfurt-am-Main, 1571. Very rare. Two of the few existing copies are in the Widener Library, Harvard University.

just king lived not under a man but under a just law—"non sunt sub homine sed sub Deo et recta lege".[1] Again and again Las Casas repeated that "he who abused authority was unworthy to rule"[2]—while implicit obedience was due to a king, to a tyrant no obedience whatever was due, and tyrannicide might become just and necessary.[3]

The rules of government which a king observes and a tyrant disregards, which distinguish between a king, the true defender of the realm, and a tyrant, its would-be proprietor, are described at great length in Las Casas' writings, and with much repetition. They fall into four principal groups. The king must provide justice and keep the peace; he must uphold and defend the Church, and support its missionary work; he must maintain and respect the rights of his subjects according to custom, including both their property and their legal "liberties", which in the medieval sense are another form of property; and he must preserve the realm and the royal authority, which is not his own, intact for his successors. All these duties were well known in the Middle Ages— Bracton, for instance, mentioned them all, including

[1] *Erudita Explicatio*, p. 17: "Habet enim super eos potestatem non suam, sed legis subjectam bono communi, ideo non sunt illi sub potestate sua sed sub potestate legis," quoted in Hanke, *Teorías políticas de B. de Las Casas*.

[2] *Entre los Remedios*, Razón X: "El que usa mal del dominio no es digno de señorear, y al tyrano ninguna fe ni obediencia ni ley se debe guardar."

[3] *Este es un Tratado*: "Cuando algún reino, pueblo o ciudad padece opresiones y molestías de algún tyrano, lo podrían los tiranizados justamente impugnar, y por librarse de su insoportable yugo, matarlo."

THE CASE AGAINST THE ENCOMIENDA

the fourth; the king might not "blemish the realm". Las Casas, however, attributed them not merely to the Spanish royal authority in its "natural realm", but to the imperial authority of a centralised monarchy in territory which it had won by conquest, and in which, according to the theory and practice of the Spanish crown, the ordinary limitations upon kingship did not exist. In this, Las Casas' theory was revolutionary. He maintained that the crown in the New World, through evil advice, had permitted its Spanish vassals, not only to infringe the liberties of its Indian subjects, but also to "blemish the realm".

The greater part of the *Erudita Explicatio*—which, significantly, was not printed until after its author's death, and then in Germany—is concerned with the question of the alienation of royal property and jurisdiction, and denies emphatically the right of a king to grant away authority over any part of his realm, or any of his subjects or their property, or to alienate any of the property of the State, or, except under exceptional circumstances, any part of the royal patrimony. Las Casas interpreted alienation in the strictest possible sense. The sale of offices was an alienation of authority, and however general it might be, was unjust and illegal. Above all, the encomienda, granting to private persons a strictly royal jurisdiction and authority over the Indians, was according to Las Casas "onerosa, injusta, tiránica, y horrible",[1] contrary to reason, natural law, and the laws of Castile.

[1] *Entre los Remedios.*

54 THE CASE AGAINST THE ENCOMIENDA

The official relation between the Spanish crown and the Indies was proprietary. The Indies were the private concern of the King, and had been so considered since Columbus' first voyage. The reprimands which Columbus received for granting and selling Indian slaves were probably prompted more by Isabella's jealousy of encroachments upon her property than by humanitarian scruples—she herself gave away Indian slaves on several occasions. Charles V had felt free to sell his claim to the Moluccas to Portugal, although the Cortes of Castile had previously extracted from him a promise that he would on no account part with the islands. The Cortes had no concern with the affairs of the Indies. Charles V was the most liberal of the Spanish monarchs of the sixteenth century. He first permitted Aragonese and Flemings to trade with the Indies; he alone set aside the commercial monopoly of Seville;[1] but even in his reign the right to visit or to trade in the New World remained a private right and continued to depend, as it did throughout the colonial period, on individual royal license.

Las Casas never accepted, or even understood, this attitude of the Crown. His whole theory rested upon the belief that the Indians, equally with the people of Spain, were the natural subjects of the Spanish Crown, and enjoyed from the moment of their entering into the Spanish obedience, all the guarantees of liberty and justice provided by the laws of

[1] Cf. R. B. Merriman, *The Rise of the Spanish Empire in the Old World and the New*, vol. III, p. 629 (New York, 1918–34).

Castile. They owed also the allegiance and the duties of Spanish subjects, and Las Casas maintained that intellectually they were fully capable of discharging those duties, and of receiving the Catholic Faith. He evolved a theory of an ideal missionary Empire in which the Indians would live immediately under their own *caciques*, subject to the authority of benevolent royal officials who would administer justice, instruct them in European customs, and discourage barbarous practices. The Church would proceed freely and peacefully with its work of conversion and spiritual ministration (Las Casas had nothing to say about the Inquisition). Europeans, as private persons, if they were to be allowed in the Indies at all, would live apart from the Indians, and live by their own labour. The Spanish Crown from time to time itself gave momentary support to such suggestions. Hundreds of prelates and missionaries and many royal officials went to the Indies with ideas in some ways similar to those of Las Casas. Almost all compromised with the conquistador class, as even the just and able Ramírez de Fuenleal was compelled to do in New Spain. The Crown eventually came to recognise the inevitability of such a course. Las Casas alone, from the time when he gave up his own encomienda, would admit no compromise.

Sepúlveda and Las Casas, whatever the original springs of their thought, represented the two divergent, yet complementary, tendencies of the imperialist theory of their time—Sepúlveda the feudal, Las Casas the constitutional and ecclesiastical.

Sepúlveda wished to interpose between the Crown and the Indians a benevolent aristocracy, who might exercise at first hand a paternal authority which the Crown could not conveniently exercise at a distance, and who would be entitled to use Indian labour in reward for their services. Las Casas wished to impose upon the Crown, in dealing with the Indians, the same limitations which, in his opinion, the law of God and the laws of Castile placed upon it in Spain. The thought of both was firmly rooted in the Middle Ages. Neither of the parties which they represented could do more than modify the policy of an irresponsible, though conscientious, absolutism—a policy which, though designed honourably to protect the mass of the American natives, inevitably destroyed the influence of their noble and priestly castes and insidiously weakened their indigenous cultures.

V

THEORY AND PRACTICE IN THE COLONIES

LAS CASAS had won a technical victory in the debates at Valladolid; his opponent's book remained unpublished until comparatively modern times, and the academic world in Spain continued to frown upon the system which Sepúlveda had supported. The theoretical victory over "Democrates" was small consolation, however, for the practical defeat which Las Casas had suffered in the matter of the abolition of the encomienda. The restrictions placed upon the re-established encomienda seemed inadequate and hopelessly difficult to enforce; yet all the eloquence of the Dominicans failed to revive the clauses of the New Laws which the Cédula of Malines had revoked, and, as if the inconclusive wordy battle had worn out the enthusiasm of both sides, the question of imperialism gradually disappeared thereafter from serious academic debate in Spain. There were still discussions upon the wisdom of allowing encomiendas to become inheritable in perpetuity; but in general, after the middle of the sixteenth century the political theory of imperialism has to be deduced from imperial practice and from the opinions of imperial administrators. The events of the decade following the promulgation of the New Laws made one thing clear: that in future the government would seek advice upon colonial policy from its servants in the colonies, not from theorists in Spain.

In the colonies theoretical argument continued. Efforts to enforce the compromise embodied in the Cédula of Malines and the decrees of 1549–1551 produced much acrimonious discussion, and some serious inquiry into the status of the Indians before the conquest.[1] Roughly the same schools of thought which had appeared at the Juntas of Valladolid were represented in the colonies, though opinions there were naturally more obviously dictated by private interest and more closely concerned with practical affairs. Naturally, too, the encomienda and all that it implied received far more general support in the colonies than in Spain, not only from the encomenderos themselves, but also from churchmen of undoubted sincerity and kindliness. Domingo de Betanzos, one of the best known of the Dominican missionaries, actually expressed the opinion that the Indians were animals, possessed of neither soul nor reason and needing, for their own good, the absolute authority of civilised masters; at one time he almost succeeded in converting Cardinal Loaysa, President of the Council of the Indians, to this heterodox view.

[1] Cf. V. de Puga, *Cedulario*, vol. II, p. 229: "Serie de preguntas con intento de basar los tributos de los Indios en los de la época gentil (1553)." M. Cuevas, ed., *Colección de documentos del siglo XVI para la historia de México*, p. 235 (Mexico, 1920): "Fray Domingo de la Anunciación respondiendo desde Chimalhuacán." H. Ternaux-Compans, ed., "Rapport sur les chefs de la Nouvelle-Espagne (Report of Alonso de Zorita)" in *Voyages, Relations et Mémoires originaux pour servir à l'histoire de la découverte de l'Amérique* (Paris, 1837–41).

Betanzos retracted upon his deathbed, and his Dominican brethren saw to it that the retraction received wide publicity;[1] a copy was sent to the Council of the Indies—an indication of the importance of the issue. Many of the clergy, however, continued to regard the Indians as irrational beings and to refuse them the sacraments in defiance of the Bull *Sublimis Deus*.

Fray Toribio Motolinía, prominent a little later in the mission field of New Spain, while holding a more orthodox view of the capacity of the Indians, upheld Betanzos' opinions concerning their treatment. His letter to the Emperor[2] written in 1555, contained an emphatic defence of the encomenderos, and carried considerable weight despite the writer's very evident dislike and jealousy of Las Casas, which rendered his evidence more than suspect. Las Casas, according to Motolinía, had exaggerated the virtues and abilities of the Indians and painted a wholly false picture of New Spain under Spanish rule; his attitude before the Junta of Valladolid reflected his own spiritual pride and his desire to be thought the Indians' only friend. Contrary to Las Casas' assertions, the Indians lived happily in encomienda, were taught Christian doctrine at the encomenderos' expense and in many places grew rich while the Spaniards remained poor; the number of slaves was decreasing rapidly and was much smaller than it had been under the Aztec

[1] Cf. L. Hanke, "Pope Paul III and the American Indians", *Harvard Theological Review* (April 1937).

[2] J. García-Icazbalceta, ed., *Documentos para la historia de México*, vol. I, p. 253 (Mexico, 1858–66).

emperors; the cruelties of the first encomenderos, which had been so notorious immediately after the conquest, had long ceased. Las Casas, in short, was an unquiet spirit who stirred up trouble wherever he went; his book (the *Brevísima Relación*) was seditious and would merely encourage the enemies of Spain. (In making this last accusation Motolinía spoke more truly than he knew.)

Las Casas had also his supporters in the Indies, however. Passing mention has already been made of Fray Gaspar de Recarte,[1] who wrote his *Tratado* towards the end of the century. There were many earlier writings, among which perhaps the most interesting for its theoretical content was an anonymous document, sent from Mexico to the Council of the Indies at about the same time as Motolinía's letter, under the title "Parecer razonado de un teólogo desconocido sobre el título del dominio del Rey de España sobre las personas y tierras de Indios".[2] The writer recapitulated the familiar arguments of Gregorio López—that the paganism of the Indians gave to the Spaniards no right to make war, "contrary to what some have taught", provided that Christians and Christian converts were not molested—and recalled the decision of the Council of Toledo forbidding the use of force in making conversions. These arguments were familiar on both sides of the Atlantic; but in dealing with the claims

[1] M. Cuevas, ed., *Colección de documentos del siglo XVI para la historia de México*, p. 356 (Mexico, 1920): "Tratado del servicio personal y repartimiento de los Indies de Nueva España, 1584."

[2] Cuevas, *op. cit.* p. 176.

of King and Pope, the author of the *Parecer razonado* moved on to more controversial ground. The Pope, he maintained, could grant no rights in the New World to any prince—"quia nemo dat quod non habet"—but could only authorise ecclesiastical missions. The Spanish missions, however, had achieved such successes that the Indians, perceiving the advantages of being governed by a Christian monarch, had enthusiastically accepted the authority of the King of Spain. Their willing acceptance, which made him their "natural sovereign", constituted the King's only title to rule in the Indies and to levy moderate tributes to cover the expenses of government. All the familiar obligations of kingship, to respect and protect the rights of subjects, were implicit in such a title. The Indians should legally retain their lands and their personal freedom. The encomienda, established for the instruction and conversion of the Indians (which should have been left to the clergy) had become an instrument of oppression and should be abolished.

Such a simple and direct political theory was unusual even for a colonial missionary. The reports and writings of overworked colonial justices and officials in the same period contained less optimistic, less logical, but far more practical opinions. Many of these men had the courage to describe conditions as they saw them and to recommend reforms which they knew to be unpopular, particularly during the administration of Luis de Velasco I in New Spain from 1550 to 1564. The definite decision having been made to allow the encomienda system to continue in a mitigated form, the viceregal court made every effort in those years to enforce humane legislation and to keep the encomenderos under ever stricter supervision.[1] Royal visitadores overran the provinces, assessing tributes, hearing complaints, freeing slaves, and annulling grants of encomienda which had expired or had been obtained by fraudulent means. Many judges, especially in remote provinces, were made to suffer for their inconvenient zeal. The career of the Licenciado Lorenzo Lebrón de Quiñones was a typical example of such effective but unpopular administration. Lebrón was a Justice of the Audiencia of New Galicia, selected by Velasco to conduct a Visita in the Province of Colima. The voluminous report which he sent to Spain at the end of four years' work[2] contains a description of the condition of the native population very different from the cheerful picture presented by Motolinía and the author of the *Parecer razonado*. The account of Lebrón's own activities includes the liberation of slaves, the annullment of illegal encomiendas, and a long list of sentences pronounced against encomenderos for ill-treating their Indians, for pasturing their flocks upon Indian land, for extorting illegal services, and for collecting tributes in excess of the assessments published by the Audiencia. The report was warmly praised by the Viceroy and by many of the clergy.[3]

[1] Cf. Zavala, S., *La Encomienda Indiana*, Madrid, 1935.
[2] *Archivo General de Indias*, Seville, Patronato 20, No. 5, R⁰ 14 (1–1–1/20).
[3] Mariano Cuevas, *Documentos...siglo XVI*, pp. 156, 205, 215.

Complaints were made, however, of Lebrón's undoubtedly high-handed methods, and as a result Lebrón and his fellow justices were themselves subjected to a Visita in which Lebrón was condemned upon trumped up charges of immorality and deprived of his judicial office. The Viceroy, though convinced of Lebrón's innocence, feared his tactlessness and dared not reinstate him, and a letter to Las Casas, from one honest reformer to another, produced no immediate result. Lebrón was driven to go to Spain and present his case in person before the Council of the Indies. He was honourably acquitted and reinstated in office, but died before reaching his post—a pathetic but significant figure. Appointed to a judicial office, he had at once been given a commission which involved his acting not only as judge, but as policeman, prosecutor, tax-gatherer, administrator, commissioner of public works (he supervised the building of many roads and bridges) and possibly hangman also. His case illustrated the combined effect of the special requirements of the colonies, and the increase of absolutism at home, upon an established and hitherto respected judicial system. Significantly, too, Lebrón, in begging the support of Las Casas, urged his claim not as a friend of the Indians (though he was that) but as a loyal servant who had striven to enforce the King's decrees.[1] Lebrón represented the type of man upon which every successful empire relies—the man who regards unquestioning obedience to orders from above as a

[1] *D.I.I.* vol. VII, p. 250.

cardinal virtue. Unthinking obedience and loyalty to an established system was rare among Spaniards at the time of the Conquest, but became more and more the essential characteristic of royal officials in the Spanish Empire, until finally it stifled all possibility of local initiative arising in the colonies.

The political theories of a loyal bureaucracy were well illustrated in the writings of several of Lebrón's contemporaries in the southern viceroyalty. Much of this secular colonial writing was of the sort nowadays described as "inspired". Francisco de Toledo, the great Viceroy of Peru, encouraged officials and judges to justify by theoretical argument the work which they performed under his authority in Peru— work which, besides honest reform, included such doubtful expedients as the judicial murder of the Inca Tupac Amarú. It was at Toledo's suggestion or command that Captain Pedro Sarmiento wrote his history of the Incas,[1] with the avowed intention of proving those rulers to be tyrants and usurpers rather than the "natural sovereigns" of Peru. Sarmiento proposed, in his dedication to Philip II, to reassure the King's conscience, unnecessarily disturbed by the carping of ill-informed theologians such as the Bishop of Chiapas. He pointed out that the most kingly of virtues was liberality; that the King of Spain, being more liberal than other monarchs, needed greater resources; that the natives of Peru had no legitimate sovereigns, being ruled by

[1] R. Pietschmann, ed., *Geschichte des Inkareiches von Pedro Sarmiento de Gamboa* (text and introduction), Berlin, 1906.

tyrants; and that the unnatural vices and human sacrifices practised by the Incas gave sufficient ground for the war of conquest which had been waged against them. The authority of Vitoria was cited in support of this last proposition. The rest of the argument was supplied by the history itself.

More interesting, from the point of view of the student of institutions, is the work of Juan de Matienzo, judge of the Royal Audiencia of Charcas, who, in the intervals of holding court in the fastnesses of the Bolivian jungle, wrote a brilliant account of the Spanish government of Peru in his own day.[1] The book contains a description of the country and its administration, and a list of the reforms which Matienzo claimed to have suggested to the Viceroy Toledo, who actually put many of them into practice. As a preface to the principal subject-matter this author also enumerated the circumstances which gave to the King of Spain the right to govern the Indies: the former tyranny of the Incas, the paganism of the Indians in general, their unnatural vices, their resistance to the Gospel, the fact that much of the land of South America lay unoccupied and idle—any of these constituted a valid and just reason for the Spanish conquest. Unlike Sarmiento, Matienzo made no attempt to assume a tone of high moral indignation in this connection; his book was not a polemic. His attitude indicated rather, that however the Indies had been gained, the King of Spain was

[1] J. de Matienzo (ed. J. N. Matienzo), *Gobierno del Perú*, Buenos Aires, 1910.

King *de facto* in America, had legislated for the government of the colonies, and needed no further title to the absolute obedience of all the inhabitants. Matienzo showed a practising lawyer's impatience with abstract political theory—an impatience which was becoming general, in the second half of the sixteenth century, throughout an Empire governed by lawyers—and an exaggerated belief in the power of law and legislation also typical of Spanish imperialism in its developed form.

The same well-defined stages can therefore be traced in the thought of the official classes in the colonies as in that of the academic world in Spain: an emphatic statement of the rights of the conquerors, countered by humanitarian arguments on behalf of the Indians; fierce debate and strenuous appeals to the Crown from all parties; finally the acceptance of a compromise evolved by the method of trial and error and imposed by the government, the humanitarian party being placated by a series of minor reforms, the influential colonists "bought off" with encomiendas of the pension type, and the Indians left more and more in the care of royal justices and officials. As might be expected, an exactly analogous process took place in the development of administrative practice in the colonies.

The reforms instituted in Peru by the Viceroy Francisco de Toledo, and recorded in Matienzo's book present a fairly complete picture of the type of compromise which the colonial government evolved after the encomienda agitation had died down.

Matienzo maintained that the most pressing evil, as far as the Indians were concerned, was not the encomienda, but the oppression of the native *Caciques*, to whom were entrusted the collection of taxes and the organisation of the *Mita*, or public labour tribute.[1] A contributory cause of misery was the fact that the Indians, from Inca times, held no land of their own, and depended upon the wages of their labour to pay their taxes.[2] In order to remedy this situation, the Viceroy appointed Corregidores in every group of villages (repartimiento) who were to supervise the allocation of tasks, the payment of wages, and the assessment of taxation. Indians between the ages of eighteen and fifty (the Peruvians, were, and are, a longlived race) owed, under Toledo's provisions, a maximum of seventy days' forced labour—forty days to their encomendero, in the case of Indians held in encomienda, and thirty days of *Mita*, or public work, the thirty days being divided into eight for the village priest, ten for the Cacique, four for the public works of the village, and eight for the King—in practice, for the Corregidor. The Corregidores were to see that the wages for all this work were paid directly to the labourers, so that the Caciques might have no opportunity for peculation. Matienzo further evolved, and Toledo attempted to apply, an elaborate scheme for dividing village lands

[1] "El Cacique es el señor natural de estos Indios y no pierde el señorío que tiene sobre ellos", *Gobierno del Perú*, cap. 10.

[2] *Ibid.* cap. 11. Compare the native situation in some parts of Africa: J. A. Hobson, *Imperialism* (London, 1902); Morel, *The Black Man's Burden* (London, 1920).

and granting to every family plots of ground which might on no account be sold to Spaniards.

The enforcement of labour dues, rather than their equivalent in kind or money, by the encomenderos continued longer in Peru than in New Spain (where commutation was fairly complete by 1550). The encomenderos had always been more powerful in Peru; they had risen and killed Blasco Núñez Vela, the first Viceregal reformer. Toledo dared not interfere too drastically with their supposed rights, at first. Even his moderate reforms aroused opposition. Armendáriz, the President of the Audiencia of Charcas, a conservative lawyer who hated Matienzo and always supported the encomenderos, wrote to the King inquiring whether Toledo's instructions were to be obeyed—"for they are so numerous and so complicated that we should require long and careful study merely to understand them".[1] He stigmatised the administration of the corregidores as a "sale of justice" and explained sourly that "the corregidor robs in order to return to Spain a rich man; and the Cacique robs to keep the corregidor quiet".[2] Armendáriz' real complaint was against the interference of an effective Viceregal administration in his province. More impartial observers remarked that the encomenderos hated Toledo because he ended their extortions; the ecclesiastics, because he curtailed their civil jurisdiction; and the judges, because he

---

[1] Levillier, *Correspondencia de la Audiencia de Charcas*, p. 286 (Buenos Aires, 1916).
[2] *Ibid.* p. 379.

interfered to prevent unnecessary litigation. The days of such men as Armendáriz were past—at least as the highest authorities in the Empire. In 1550, the Council of the Indies could still declare that "The most serious obligation which Your Majesty owns in the government of the new lands of the Indies, is to provide an abundance of justice...".[1] Las Casas wrote in the same strain, but twenty years later only a confirmed conservative would have defined the duties of the sovereign in such medieval terms. Matienzo spoke of the Appeal Court of which he was a judge, not as the fount of justice but as the "principal wall and defence" of its province. Already in his day, the administrative work of the Audiencias occupied more time and energy than did the hearing of appeals; the courts were becoming administrative boards, employed in carrying into practice the decrees of the King and the Viceroy. The régimes of Velasco in New Spain, of Toledo in Peru, showed that legislation and administration were to be the essential activities of colonial government; and that the old, respected judicial authority associated with the early Audiencias, in Spain and in America, was inadequate for the government of a vast colonial empire.

[1] Levillier, *Correspondencia de la Audiencia de Charcas*, p. 503.

VI

IMPERIALISM AND SOVEREIGNTY

A JUDICIAL system, even if it be worked by men of superhuman impartiality, and shielded from all suggestion of political influence, cannot function without an established body of law which it may apply. The Audiencias could not have been expected to apply Indian notions of right and law, even had they understood them. On the other hand, the notions of right and law which grew out of early colonial custom were felt by almost all thinking Spaniards to be thoroughly evil. A thoroughly conquered people, in effect, has no legal rights except those granted to it, as of grace, by the conquerors; while the conquerors claim a new set of rights which require legal definition, with reference to new responsibilities. There is no "Common Law"—in the absence of an international legislative body—which can cover the needs of both peoples (if the conquered race survives) and which can justify the establishment of judicial institutions such as the Audiencias. A new situation calls for legislation—no system of philosophy or body of custom will serve, as Matienzo realised though Las Casas and Sepúlveda did not; and legislation, to be effective and convincing, requires the assumption of sovereignty.

That assumption was made, in practice, at the

beginning of the colonial era, when the Crown began to issue colonial decrees which (unlike medieval legislation) made no pretence of being declaratory, and which neither received nor required any constitutional consent. These Cédulas, far from being limited by an existing system of rights, avowedly created new rights and abolished supposedly established ones. Much of this legislation was, in intention at least, enlightened according to the standards of the time; much, in the first sixty years, was based upon the opinions of some of the best thinkers and theologians in Spain; much again, upon reasonably accurate reports of colonial conditions and requirements. All, however, was arbitrary, sanctioned by the royal will alone, tempered only by the difficulties of enforcement at a distance. The New Laws of 1542, the various Ordenanzas sobre Descubrimiento, and above all the great Colonial Code—the "Recopilación de Leyes de las Indias"—form the most impressive of all monuments to an absolute imperial sovereignty based upon the formal assumption that the Indies were the private estate of the rulers of Castile.

The feeling (not at first the formal theory) of sovereignty thus entered Spanish government as it were by the back door. The proprietary theory, in any naked form, would never have been tolerated in Spain; but in the Indies, fiction though it was, it enabled the Crown to exercise a maximum of political authority with a minimum of political responsibility and tended to produce an idea of sovereignty much nearer to that sponsored by the later English publicist, Sir Robert Filmer, than to the native notion of a sovereignty limited by "constituent law", as evolved by the Spanish juridical school. This sterile sovereignty, untempered even by constitutional forms, could not be confined indefinitely to the colonies. The Crown had grown accustomed to employing absolutist formulae in the government of the Indies, and to following an absolutist practice by which the important institutions there, judicial, ecclesiastical, economic and local, became converted into one vast centralised civil service, designed to enforce arbitrary legislation. The theory and practice of government in Spain could not remain long unaffected. Only a very drastic decentralisation could have saved the Spain which the writers of the juridical school so admired; but such a course was only once suggested seriously to the government, and then by a Dutchman, Fray Nicholas de Witte, a trusted friend of the Emperor, who wrote to his sovereign in 1552 recommending the appointment of a prince of the blood to govern the Indies independently of Spain.[1] de Witte argued that "distant possessions are the most easily lost"; but in fact it was Spain which was "lost."—exhausted by an effort too great for the Spaniards' meagre resources.

Absolutism and imperialism both inevitably impose heavy financial burdens upon the subjects of the states affected by them, and imperial govern-

[1] *Algunos documentos de la Colección Cuevas*, Mexico, 1924, Carta al Emperador, 1552.

ments naturally look to their colonies for an income which may relieve the strain at home. In the Spanish Empire especially, enactments concerning the *Real Hacienda* occupied a disproportionate place in colonial legislation, and the supervision of treasury officials was early added to the multifarious duties of the royal Audiencias. Both Spaniards and foreigners probably exaggerated the importance of the New World revenue in relation to the total royal income. The bullionist theory of the time approved the accumulation of silver and ignored its baneful effects, both upon currency and prices, and upon royal policy.[1] Danger was aggravated by the rigidity of the economic structure of Spain, and its inability to adapt itself to the needs of a colonial market. In 1552 it was even proposed to prohibit the export of various manufactured articles, in order to prevent a further rise in prices.[2]

Economic conditions such as these could not fail to exert a demoralising influence upon the constitutional government of Spain. As early as 1524 the Cortes of Castile protested against the proposal to sell the Moluccas to Portugal, on the ground that the possession of the Spice Islands secured to the Emperor a steady income, independent of taxation. The deputies, in fact, were prepared to relinquish their only political bargaining counter—the control

[1] Cf. E. J. Hamilton, *American Treasure and the Price Revolution in Spain* (Harvard, 1934).

[2] Cf. C. de Lannoy and H. Van der Linden, *Histoire de l'expansion coloniale des peuples européens* (Brussels, 1907), Portugal et Espagne, p. 424 and references there.

of financial supplies—in order to relieve the burden under which they and their countrymen laboured. According to the economic theories of the time the argument was reasonable; but it augured ill for the constitutional future of Spain. The old constitutional instinct was weak already; the development of imperialism completed its extinction.

In the purely physical sense, Spain was more vulnerable to the growth of absolutism than the colonies themselves. In the Indies great distances, a difficult terrain and racial prejudice presented formidable obstacles to the royal will, as the failure to enforce the New Laws clearly showed. The formula "obedézcase pero no se cumpla", while respectfully accepting absolutist law and theory, indicated that in practice royal decrees were not always effective. In Spain, physical obstacles were far less evident; as soon as Spaniards lost their pride in the "fueros of Castile"—the liberties of municipalities, the rights of the Cortes—then Spain became doomed to a bureaucratic absolutism more complete than that which prevailed in the colonies.

Students of imperialism after the middle of the sixteenth century had abandoned in despair their attempt to persuade the Crown to recognise some system of constitutional rights in the New World. Similarly, the writers of the Spanish juridical school, all earnest champions of constitutional sovereignty, could not ignore for ever the glaring contradiction between their theories and the practice of the state in which they lived. The school did not long survive

IMPERIALISM AND SOVEREIGNTY

the sixteenth century, and its later representatives, especially Mariana, wrote with a sad recognition of fading glories. Imperialism, more than any other single cause, killed the best political thought of Spain, as it tends eventually to kill all forms of thought.